D1383395

Memento Mori

Also by the author

Picnic on the Moon
(Leapfrog Press)

All Sins Forgiven: Poems for My Parents
(Leapfrog Press)

Poems

Memento Mori

Charles Coe

Leapfrog Press
Fredonia, New York

Cover photo © Gordon Webster, New England Image LLC
Sculpture by Ann Hirsch
Author photo © Gordon Webster

Published in 2019 in the United States by
Leapfrog Press LLC
PO Box 505
Fredonia, NY 14063
www.leapfrogpress.com

Printed in the United States of America

Distributed in the United States by
Consortium Book Sales and Distribution
St. Paul, Minnesota 55114
www.cbsd.com

First Edition

Library of Congress Cataloging-in-Publication Data

Names: Coe, Charles, 1952- author.
Title: Memento mori : poems / Charles Coe.
Description: First edition. | Fredonia, New York : Leapfrog Press, 2019.
Identifiers: LCCN 2018049937 | ISBN 9781948585026 (paperback : alk. paper)
Subjects: LCSH: American poetry–21st century.
Classification: LCC PS3553.O338 A6 2019 | DDC 811/.54–dc23
LC record available at https://lccn.loc.gov/2018049937

"Use your numbered days to throw open the windows of your soul to the sun. If you do not, the sun will soon set, and you with it."
—Marcus Aurelius, *The Emperor's Handbook*

Contents

Memento Mori

Part I

Inventory (for the poets of Norfolk Correctional Institution)

As a child I tried to keep track of certain things:
cracks in the sidewalk between the bus stop and school,
names of streets between the bridge and our family's house,
toy soldiers lined up on a shelf

Now the list of things I've lost, or forgotten,
or thrown away, at times seems longer
than the list of what remains.
Sometimes this feeling visits uninvited, late at night,
when every breath is a footstep
measuring the miles till dawn.

But this gray morning as I walked across the yard,
the sun suddenly shoved through the clouds
to warm my face, and later I was graced
by a small kindness from an unexpected source.

This is not the life I would have chosen.
But I will try to keep an open hand
for the gifts it spreads each day across my path,
like Easter eggs hidden in the grass.

For the Ancient Boston Bar with Neon Shamrocks in the Windows, Recently Departed

Years ago one rainy afternoon
I wandered into the bar
in search of a pay phone.

Scattered in the gloom
a dozen pairs of eyes
as cold and hard as Irish granite
glanced up and settled
on my dark skin.

I know that in the proper circumstance
anyone there might have been delighted
to crack my skull.

Even so, I've seen enough
of what I thought was mine slip away
that when I pass their old haunt
with its shiny new façade
and the flock of brightly plumed
young revelers whose mating calls
fill the night, I can't help but feel a twinge.

Loss makes brothers of us all.

Dance

Under the loving touch of our lead-footed conductor, the Red Line train lurches toward the Charles Street platform like a cat coughing up a hairball. And we, this carful of impatient jostled mammals, we're the hairballs, with our shiny phones and the five-dollar eggplant/radicchio lattes we're trying so hard not to spill. The train stops for half a minute, jerks into motion for six or seven feet, and then with what seems like a final, expiring sigh, stops again. And stays stopped.

So we're stuck on this cold, gray Monday morning, lodged deep in the alimentary canal of another New England winter, while the sky spits a mutant mix of rain and snow and frogs and gravel and broken toasters and shards of radioactive broken glass. Everything and everybody seems pissed; the conductor seems pissed, the Charles River seems pissed, its frozen face streaked with jagged cracks. Even the ducks sitting on the ice seem pissed–maybe because they're in Massachusetts and not Mexico, or because they're sitting on a river named after a second-rate English King.

As the unmoving moments turn to minutes, when I tire of contemplating geese, my attention wanders toward a young girl standing nearby whose lips and hair are the same color purple. I tune into her conversation with two young guys that at first sounds friendly, but as it quickly becomes clear the guys are competing over her. On second thought, they're not exactly competing, it's more like one guy taking verbal jabs at the other with a hostility his glued-on smile can't disguise. But the other fellow's warding off the jabs with the subtlety and sly humor of vintage Muhammed Ali. He might not be trying to compete but he's definitely scoring points; he and the girl begin exchanging little conspiratorial glances.

The first guy tries to keep his cool, but he's starting to get pissed and it seems that if he had just little room to move he might actually start hopping up and down like the ducks on the ice, flapping his arms to keep her attention.

Suddenly, at least for the moment, it's all ok: the lousy weather, the lead-footed conductor, the excruciating commute, the briefcase that keeps poking me in the back. It's all ok, as I stand on this unmoving train, suspended in space above the frozen river, watching these three beautiful not-quite children dance the oldest dance in the world.

Sermon

Driving in the rain late one night and fiddling with the radio, I stumbled across a Haitian Creole station with a preacher in mid sermon, voice pouring from the speakers in a full-throated, rhythmic roar, extolling the glories of salvation.

Perhaps at that very moment some lost soul was pulling to the side of the road, rain pouring down his windshield, surrendering grief and fear and guilt in a torrent of tears, forehead against the steering wheel, while in the little studio the preacher kept calling listeners to 'Jezi Kri'– Jesus Christ, eyes shut tight, shirt collar open, tie loose, drops of saliva baptizing the microphone.

And behind him on the wall, the hands of a clock traveling their endless orbit . . . marking the minutes of this mortal life.

The Dance Hall at Porter Square

Near the entrance to the Porter Square subway stop
is a small tree-shaded concrete plaza, off to the side
where street people congregate
and where yesterday I heard an old boombox
call out that it was "Time to get together, and love
one another right now," and saw a shirtless young man
in a grimy Red Sox cap hold out his hand
to a young woman who at first
only smiled and shook her head
as if embarrassed to be asked to dance
in such a place, or because life on the street
had already taught that joy is not to be trusted,
or maybe, because she'd just never learned to dance
in that old-fashioned way,
where two people hold each other
as he was offering to hold her now
an offer that seemed courtly, not seductive,
letting her come to him if she chose
which she did, finally,
like a shy maiden at a country fair
to take the offered hand,
and I was tempted to stop and watch
but some flowers bruise when touched
so I just kept walking, while they fumbled for,
then found, their common rhythm and a flock
of pigeons fluttered their wings in applause.

Taking Down the Tree

A massive tree, dead and leafless,
surrounded by men in hard hats and goggles,
gathered like wolves around an ancient bull elk
feeding chunks of the carcass into a voracious chipper,
cars squeezing slowly past, drivers staring at the spectacle.

An old man walking his dog has stopped to watch.
He leans against a fence, arms folded, face unreadable,
while the dog sniffs the air and looks on, curious,
at the ghosts of a billion leaves that float in a slow circle
drifting on the cool morning breeze.

exodus haiku

under the oak tree
leaves on rainwater puddle
gaze up at lost home

Yardwork

On the grounds of a Brattle Street
Tory Roy mansion two men are working,
short and squat, broad-chested, bow-legged,
so alike they could be brothers,
Aztec warriors reincarnate
who in a distant past marched
shoulder-to-shoulder terrorizing the southern plains
clad in quilted cotton armor, wooden helmets festooned
with the symbols of the fierce jaguar or eagle clan.

Now one lifts a large plant from the bed of a pick-up truck,
corded muscles flexing as he lowers the heavy pot onto a cart.

The other, with arms that once wielded the
Maquahuitl, the massive wooden sword lined with
razor-sharp obsidian that conquistadors
claimed could behead a horse with a single stroke,
spreads mulch beneath a hydrangea bush
his rake moving in a slow meditation
his ancient face quiet and still.

Poem for an Absent Friend
(for Jeff)

On a sunny day in early spring
we're on a bench at Boston Common
while you tell me the news,
which isn't good, and nibble a granola bar.

You're wearing a brand-new, chocolate-brown
Sam Spade fedora, which you remove
to reveal your head, hairless and pale,
and I imagine the radiation glowing through your skin,
the chemicals rushing through your veins
like dogs chasing a rabbit they will never catch.

An insistent squirrel chatters at our feet;
you toss a morsel of granola
then wrap the unfinished bar,
stuff it in your bag and rise.
There's somewhere else you have to be,
somewhere else, where you'll shave
another slice of time from your ever-shrinking pie.

So we walk across the Common,
past pigeons pecking in the grass
that scatter before the lion-hearted toddler's
charge, past the piper whose ancient call to battle
bounces unheeded off the blank faces
of high-rise condos, past beautiful young women
in spring finery who will offer their bodies
as gifts for someone else to unwrap,

and you're taking it all in on this farewell
tour of the world, taking it in and letting it go.

A young couple near the fountain holds a baby.
An older woman with a camera clicks the shutter
as we pass and we are captured in the frame.

Perhaps a hundred years from now
someone flipping through a dusty scrapbook
will pause a moment to contemplate our faded images,
two ancient and mysterious ghosts.

House Money

Two elderly black men navigating the crowded sidewalk
on canes stop to greet each other, exchange a handshake
complicated as a physics midterm.
"Hey man," one exclaims. "I ain't seen you in a dog's age!
What's happenin'?"

"Well, I'm still alive," his friend replies, pauses with a comic's timing
then adds, "And they still tryin' to kill me."

They laugh and shake their heads in shared awareness,
two old black men in America who've beaten the odds.

Now they're playing with house money.

Sonnet for the Young Woman
Who Offered Me Her Seat on the Train

Your smile illuminates the gloomy morn
As sunlight warms a chilly mountain lake
Before me sits a beauty not yet born
When decades trailed already in my wake
You stir as if to rise and yield your place
But I return your smile and shake my head
While hoping in the moment that my face
Will show no hint of all my thoughts unsaid
I could have sung your mother lullabies
Though still a young man lingers in my heart
Who once delighted in a young girls sighs
The time has passed for him to play that part
He read his lines upon a satin stage
But as they will the years have turned the page

Measure Twice, Cut Once
(for Tom on his 50th Birthday)

Music sleeps inside the grain
of every piece of wood, waiting
to wakened by the singing blade.

Not every ear can hear it.
For some, the slightly crooked shelf,
the rough-fitted joint that snags the shirt in passing
are good enough.

As a young man you were sometimes impatient,
anxious for the job to be done, the floor swept,
the weekend started, but now you take your time
and build to last.

The builder shapes and is shaped by
the wood, each becoming
what was always meant to be.

Ceremony

In ancient times when I was young and strong
and paid the rent by painting houses
a certain diner was a favorite breakfast spot
for those in the building trades.

But one morning we arrived to find the doors
wide open with no kitchen crew in sight,
just a gang of laborers, pallbearers
in work boots, loading benches and coolers
into a truck while we dazed regulars
huddled in the cold.

Someone spit and shook his head.
"Gonna be a chicken joint," he muttered.
"How much chicken can you eat"?

Then we noticed downy feathers
drifting to the sidewalk,
looked up to see a red-tailed hawk
perched under the roof
enjoying its own breakfast,
a fat pigeon whose lifeless body jerked
as the raptor fed.

We stood on that busy street
transfixed by the bloody feast
tongues stilled on this ordinary
morning by so much death
without warning or ceremony,
our hungry mouths open
like the beaks of orphaned baby birds.

Part II

Bowling with the Pope

The Bishop of Rome needs this spare.

But it's the dreaded seven-ten split,
the toughest shot in the game
and not one to rush.

But he isn't rushing; on the contrary,
he's quite relaxed. He always seems relaxed
when he bowls; maybe because
the rules are simple here:
no cigar smoking, no bare feet with
bowling shoes let the person
on the next lane roll first,
and most important: Leave your resume at the door.

In the world outside the frantic army of
handlers and advisors from whom he has
temporarily escaped will greet his eventual return
with relief and gratitude, whisk him off
in a limo to his next engagement,
but first things first:

He toes the line, lifts the ball
takes a deep breath, lips moving
(perhaps in prayer) as he sweeps
the satin robe aside to free his arm,
and steps smoothly into motion.

The ball hits the oak with a quiet "thunk,"

rolls down the lane in an elegant curve,
and just catches the outside edge of the seven pin
which somersaults like a circus acrobat
and plows through the ten.

The man in the next lane grins appreciatively
and the Holy Father favors him with a nod
as he strolls back to our table and takes a
casual sip from his bottle of Bud.

Christ preached humility, said all who serve him
should walk lightly, be not puffed with pride
at worldly accomplishments.

But it's hard to be humble
when you've just knocked down
a seven-ten split; I can't help noticing
my opponent's faint Madonna smile
as he picks up the stubby red pencil
to scratch in his score.

"Nice shot, your holiness," I
summon the grace to say
though it means that tonight
the pizza and beer are on me.

will you kiss me now?
(for E.E. Cummings)

so will you kiss me now?
beneath the mintgreen glow of
trees awash with baby leaves?

fiddlehead ferns curled in sleep
await their turn, have forgotten
more songs of spring than you or I
could ever learn.

will you kiss me now?
as dragonflies skate a pas de deux
upon a pond of liquid ice?

so nice to see the forest
shed the old brown coat,
turn once more to face the sun.

frogs awakening in the mud
are announcing that the
world has just begun.
so will you kiss me now?

and now?

. . . and now?

Ascension

It wasn't the milk chocolate skin of the girl behind the cash register
that forty years ago might have set our game in motion, skin untouched
by wrinkles, those dry river beds
that mark the flow of passing years.

It wasn't the ancient eyes s wise as Nefertiti's.

It was the way she took my money. When our hands were as close
to touching as they will ever be there was no pull, no tug. I simply
opened my hand and the bill floated skyward through plaster and steel
and roofing shingles, ascending to that place of which all money
dreams, forever free of human striving and desire.

cat haiku

if i were bigger
i would be licking your bones
sweet and gleaming white

haiku for apocalypse

meteors and fire
pouring down from scarlet skies
there goes the new roof

The Night My Sister Danced with a Mouse

The night my sister danced with a mouse began like an ordinary Sunday evening. My parents were in the kitchen sipping coffee and taking a break from their kids. My sister, Carol, and I were in the living room, polishing off our Swanson Frozen Turkey TV dinners and watching that guy on the Ed Sullivan show spin dinner plates on the end of sticks while the orchestra charged through "The Hungarian Fire Dance." Just as each wobbly plate seemed about to tumble off its stick and crash to Earth, he'd give a little flick with his finger to keep it spinning.

Little did we know that while we sat entranced by Plate Man's battle with gravity, a little brown mouse was creeping across the living room, headed for an epic struggle of its own, a struggle that commenced when Carol glanced down, noticed it tugging at the cuff of her pajama bottom, and levitated (no other verb will do) off the sofa. The startled mouse headed north instead of south, scrabbling up the inside of Carol's pants.

"Aggggh! Get it out! Get it out! Get it out!" she screamed, and tried to evict her uninvited guest with a series of improvised dance steps that had James Brown seen, he would have given up show biz and opened a hardware store. I can't swear her feet ever touched the floor.

When I realized what was happening I fell off the sofa and rolled around on the floor, gasping for air. At the time Carol was thirteen, and four years younger I was a card-carrying member of the Annoying Little Brother's Club.

When our parents ran in from the kitchen to see what the fuss was about, they were greeted by the sight of their daughter, an airborne, wild-eyed dervish, and their son, stretched out on the carpet–flopping like a beached bluefish. The show ended when the mouse finally dropped from Carol's pants and zoomed out of the living room–a near invisible brown blur.

Over the years The Night my Sister Danced with a Mouse became part of our family's personal mythology, a shorthand reminder that we were connected by gravitational fields of laughter and memory in ways we were connected to no one else, that we were not merely four plates spinning off in our separate and solitary dances.

Distant Replay

At a dinner party where a sing-along has broken out
an adolescent boy is embarrassed beyond endurance
when his mother warbles folk songs in a voice
unrelated to any particular key.

Someday when childhood is a distant memory
if you ask "Of all the things you can never have,
what would you want the most right now?"
He might stare into space a moment and say:

"To hear my mother sing 'Home on the Range' out of tune."

Terror Incognito: A Comedy in Three Acts

Act I: Diagnosis

I can't help noticing the doctor's tie.

It's paisley,
which I usually detest,
but this one's relatively tasteful:
muted-gold paramecia
floating peacefully on a silken lake
of indigo and forest green.
It's a tie I can almost imagine
wearing (if mildly sedated).

The tie is twisted
with the tag facing me. I try to read the label
without being obvious but the lettering's just
a little out of range so I give up and lean back
in the moderately comfortable chair
and as he continues adding
strange new words to my rapidly growing
medical vocabulary I'm listening carefully,
but at the same time I want to tell him
to straighten his tie.
I realize, however, this wouldn't fit
the moment's mood.

On the wall behind him is a framed photograph
of three young children standing in front of a canoe
by a lake, their smiles filled with summer
and the smell of pine.

"Your children," I ask?
"No," he replies, all business.
"I share this office
with another doctor."

Obviously not one for small talk,
he goes on to describe
how the expedition into my brain will proceed;
I start to picture a tiny Lewis and Clark,
striking out in their own canoe to plumb
the virgin territory of my pituitary gland
paddling mightily against rivers of red
resting each night on the banks of
arterial streams, recording their journey
in microscopic notebooks.

Finally, when he leans over to hand me an
"informational pamphlet," his twisted tie
flips around to right itself.

I decide to take this as a good omen.

Act Two: The Main Event

The nurse slips the catheter into my arm
and pumps in "a little something to calm me down"
before we head off to the operating room.
When it kicks in as my gurney slides silently
through the hospital labyrinth
I have an excellent view up her nostrils;
I can count the individual hairs.

I enjoy this view for awhile, then my attention
wanders toward the ceiling
and I realize hospital ceilings
are seriously underutilized; just think
how the cost of medical care might be defrayed
if that space was rented for advertising;
while being carted around patients could learn
of all the wonderful goods and services
those of us who survived our operations
would have the opportunity to enjoy.

And while I'm planning the ad campaign
that will revolutionize the health care industry
the clear plastic mask appears and slips
over my face, softly, like a mother's touch
that eases me into the cool and quiet dark.

Act Three: After the Show

On this sunny Saturday afternoon in early fall
on my first tentative, unassisted post-surgical outing
Harvard Square is a Fellini movie.
The clown who approaches me
is right out of central casting: striped shirt,
baggy pants with suspenders, bulbous red plastic nose.
Clutching a battered, folded top hat, he says,
 "Excuse me sir, would you like to buy a headpiece?
It's overpriced and poorly made."
I glance down. "Yes, very nice," but it
would probably just slip off my bald head."
He pursed his lips. "Have you tried Rogaine?"
"No, not my style. But I've considered Astroturf."
He grins and runs a hand through his polyester Afro.
 "Bright green? Like mine?"
"Of course," I reply. I reach for my wallet
and hand him a dollar "I like your nose."
"I like yours too," he says, then palms the bill,

I continue on my way,
shaking my head at our exchange
when suddenly the sounds and colors
start to swirl around me, tears roll
down surprised cheeks, and I hear
a whispered voice, my own, say again and again:

"You're still here. . . ."

Errata

Last Saturday's holiday cookie baking demonstration took place
at Bill's Discount Pantry: NOT Bill's Discount Panties
as previously reported in these pages.

Our apologies.

The featured presentation at the recent Church of the Redeemer's
potluck supper was a slide show of Pastor Dilford's trip to the
Holy Land: NOT a black mass featuring virgin sacrifice and an
altar covered with naked bodies writhing in a pool of mud.

We stand corrected.

We have reported that the purchase of goods and services
advertised in these pages will lead without fail to happiness,
health, and long life,

that your leaders are always wise, and pure, and true,
and rule in accordance with the high ideals upon which
our nation was founded,

that your government and military are universally loved and
respected, and welcomed with open arms in every corner of the world.

The management apologizes for these errors, and sincerely
regrets any inconvenience or confusion they may have caused.

Saga of the Fish Sticks

Driven by an ancient impulse
the fish sticks swim upstream
towards those who eagerly await
the Friday Lenten rendezvous.

The other fish, those with tails
and fins, giggle as the odd
shapes struggle past, yet the fish sticks
pay no mind, just push forward,
ever forward, while those who wait
gaze across the rolling waters
and shout with joy when the exhausted
travelers finally make their way to shore.

But just as the fish sticks think they've
shown the world who's boss . . .
their saga ends in tartar sauce.

hummingbirds   (for E.E. Cummings)

acrobatic clowns, captains of the breeze,
your graceful windborne dance
mocks my stiff-jointed shuffle.

how turgid must I seem to you,
a brontosaurus tromping through
the piney woods, a greatgray shadowcloud
across the sun.

some moonlit night would you whisper
in my earthbound ear the music
of your eyeblink heartbeat?

would you teach me how to feast
on bugs and blossom nectar
while gravity lies brooding in the grass?

this shell of mine now sags and creaks
just like an ancient porch.
someday soon, when they all think
I've left this world behind they'll cast sad eyes
upon some patch of ground but they'll
not find me there; I'll be with you,
sailing waves of wind, wings dipped
in rainbow ink,

I think.

A Woman's Laughter

On a recording of the Bill Evans trio,
Live at the Village Vanguard,
late June '61, during a slow, haunting version
of "I Loves You Porgy," at the quietest moment,
in the background, soft but clear,

a woman's laughter.

At first the sound seems jarring, even sacrilegious.
But then again a jazz club's not a concert hall,
listeners in polite rows, knees together,
waiting to cough in the space between movements.
Jazz is cash registers and clinking glasses
and chairs scraping the floor.

And besides it's a pleasant laugh, full of promise.
Easy to see her hand reach out to rest on her
companion's arm. Easy to catch the whiff of lilac or lavender . . .
Always, so many worlds within worlds.

In one world,
A man who follows Evans from gig to gig
sits at the bar alone, transfixed,
ice melting in the forgotten drink.

In one world,
The bartender counts his cash
while dreaming of the waitress's embrace.

In one world,
A woman's laughter.

In one world,
Evans leans over the keys, oblivious to all
but the slow heartbeat bass,
the splash of brushes on cymbal and snare,
fingers poised for what seems like forever
before they settle gently on the final chord.

Drummer: Chicago, 1971

Hell yeah, I remember Johnnie,
big black hands
wrapped 'round them sticks
like a second skin,
sitting on that high seat
bent over his kit
under the bright white lights.

Jesus Lord them white folks would
stomp and scream, while the black folks
sat real quiet, sipping beer
and cheap watered whiskey.

Johnny would look at those happy
pink faces, then he'd look at the
black ones kinda funny, like he
wanted something he didn't
know how to ask for.

But after awhile he
didn't look at nobody
'cause that sweat would
sting his eyes so he'd shut 'em tight . . .
and just keep workin'.

When a White Boy Plays the Blues

A white boy who plays the blues
for a black audience
is like a brother pulled over
for "Driving While Black,"
an immediate object of suspicion.

When a particular tall, skinny white boy
took the stand on a particular Chicago
summer night in a particular neighborhood club
with cheesy, splintered fake wood paneling
and sputtering neon beer sign
in the window (two of the letters burned out),
in this joint where no fresh-faced logo-covered tourists
lined up outside for a taste of blues Disneyland
the brothers waited with folded arms
to see what he could do.

We didn't care about chops;
any pimply faced first-year
conservatory student can play rings
around Muddy Waters. We were listening
not for notes, but for music.
And if he turned out to be a pretender,
we were looking for clues to identify
the specific nature of the crime.

But when he started playing we were
surprised; the notes that poured from
his guitar and throat weren't dazzling,

but they were true—water from
some well we couldn't find on a map
but we recognized the taste
so we clapped after the first tune
and he glanced at his drummer
with pleasure and relief.

As his set went on, and he got looser,
folks started to clap and grin.
The waitress at the bar
did a little two-step shuffle while she waited
for her drinks; some guy with a gold tooth
played percussion on a beer bottle with a set of keys.

The verdict was in. It was clear we all belonged in this place,
on this hot night, with our cold beers, that we were all
in our own ways outsiders, together,
faces pressed to the glass of the American Dream.

Part III

Part III

The Toll Taker's Ghost

A spectral figure sits at the edge of a cliff,
gazing down at the long gray ribbon,
far below, that winds its way through a sea of green,
through valleys, over and around hills,
skirting forests and lakes. Along the ribbon
flows an endless stream of shiny metal objects,
every color of the rainbow, slowing
then speeding up again, following
some unknowable impulse.

The figure on the cliff dimly recalls,
like visions from a memory or a dream
being keeper of an ancient temple where
the shiny objects once would pause,
recalls reaching out a hand
to gather tribute, a gesture repeated endlessly
while temple lights that flashed endlessly from red to green,
granted passage, offering blessings for the journey.

Now that temple is gone, vanished in an instant.
No trace, not a scar on the land remains.

The figure atop the cliff now waits for nothing,
simply watches the shiny objects below hurtle
along on their endless and mysterious journeys.

migrations

at season's end
the sky becomes
a river of wings.

When the Rains Came

Father, I remember that heat wave
when after six stifling days and nights
we sat together on the front porch
with a clunky old box fan that gave little relief
bare feet and bare chests, our
raggedy shorts the only nod to modesty.

Then suddenly the sky darkened,
a cool breeze ruffled the oak leaves
and a trap door opened in the belly of the clouds.

I'd rather not remember you
dragging in after your shift at the
Chevy plant, making your way from
the driveway to the front door slowly,
as if bracing yourself for the charged air
of that little gray house.

I'd rather remember you on that porch,
when we watched in wonder as one thing
became another, both of us like children,
breathing in together the evanescent smell
of cool rain kissing the hot, dry earth.

Independence Day

you could not have expected silence
after dawn's orange flame
unsealed my frozen lips.

you could not have expected stillness
knees touching in a chaste kiss
hands lying in my lap
like little brown mice.

the day rang out too clear and blue
with a million million voices
carrying the call.

so we are rising now, as one,
the moment surging though our veins
and we will dance the gray
from your bedraggled streets.

you could not have expected
all the budding blossoms in the fields
to remain asleep
beneath this fierce yellow sun.

Sometimes Brown, Sometimes Green

This time the soldiers' uniforms were brown. It was a fine, rich brown that carried well the dust of the road. The soldiers marched, shoulder to shoulder, proud, young and strong, through what was left of the town square, marched past fires that smoldered still, smoke rising lazily from the rubble, as if having burned all day and all night they had finally tired of burning.

The soldiers gathered us, we few who remained, to listen to their leader speak. He had a strong, clear voice, and spoke with fine words to explain how fortunate we were his brave soldiers had come to protect us from the common enemy.

Had his words were bread they would have filled our empty bellies.

That night my daughter slipped quietly from our battered house, so quietly that had I slept her footsteps would not have wakened me. But I was not asleep, though I kept my breathing deep and even, and my face turned to the wall as she left, and when she returned. In the morning our eyes did not meet as she added to the pot the rice and bits of dried meat she brought back from the soldiers' camp.

At the last moon, at harvest time, the soldiers' uniforms were green. They gathered us to listen to their leader speak. He had a strong, clear voice, and used many fine words to explain how fortunate we were his brave soldiers had come to protect us from the common enemy.

We stood silently as soldiers in uniforms the color of locusts carried off the sacks of our newly harvested grain. Their leader said we should be proud that the fruit of our labor and land would be used to aid the great cause.

Now, brown soldiers have defeated the green. Today a fallen green lay outside my door. His ruined face showed neither pain nor anger, only surprise that his leader's fine words could not protect him from the enemy's might.

When the last soldier stares with sightless eyes into the sun, when the houses have all burned to the ground, when the scorched earth is finally stripped bare and the only crops it holds are the bodies of our children, then let the ghosts of buglers take the field
to sound the victory call there is no one left to hear.

Billy Pilgrim Reflects
(for Kurt Vonnegut)

I never talk about it:
Sometimes sitting in the yard
with a few friends
as the grill settles
to an ash-covered glow
I'm tempted but as always,
I'm silent.

Last night I dreamed of flame and smoke,
bullets and bombs,
woke in a sweat, reached
across the bed for comfort
but was startled by the unfamiliar
shape of my wife's breast,
realized it was a different breast
I'd been reaching for.

So I rose, walked outside
searched the sky for a certain star
too far away for the naked eye
my mind aswirl with memories of golden light,
of walls and ceilings made of glass
of the endless parade of quiet, curious faces.

In the end, every circle will be closed.
Something waits for me,
waits for you, with sharp and bloody fangs,
just beyond the fire's glow.
But for now I gaze at a sky full of stars

feel the breeze against my face
and breathe in the crickets' serenade
on this never-to-be-repeated summer night.

Arion's Song

Arion was a famous singer of ancient Greece, returning home after a lucrative tour of the Mediterranean on a ship commanded by a captain who coveted his wealth.

When our captain said, "We shall feed you
to the fish and have your gold,"
Arion raised a hand.
"First, grant one wish . . . that
I may sing a final song." The captain
grinned and shrugged. "As you will."

But when the man began to sing
a sound rolled over me
such as I had never heard,
dark and deep as the ocean,
wave after wave, a sound that
brought back every joy, every sorrow

I had ever known to take hold
of me anew, wave after wave,
the sound of my beating heart,
of the blood rushing through my veins.

When the song ended
I was washed clean,
no longer what I had been
mere moments before.
I looked about me at shipmates
who stood stunned, as I was stunned,

trees rooted to the oaken deck,

all but the captain who with face
like a fist, nodded to order
the singer tossed into the sea.
Yet before any could put hand to him
the singer leapt overboard and plunged
into the churning black water.

My spirits sank as well,
but were lifted when he rose
like Poseiden on the back of a dolphin
that had been charmed by his song
and bore him safely to shore.

We men leaned over the side to watch,
tears mixing with the salt spray
that splashed our faces,

as he vanished from our sight.

The Bells of the Basilica
(for Mission Hill Church)

When the bells of the Basilica toll the hour,
a river of sound flows down Tremont Street.

It flows over the donut shop,
the pizza parlors, the post office,
the hardware store.
It flows over the Asian woman
who sits waiting for the bus, her ancient,
wrinkled face the map of a world
to which she will never return.

it flows over teenaged girls
released from the bondage of school,
who chatter in Spanish like colorful,
land-locked birds.

It flows over the college man
who wanders into traffic
staring at his phone.

The bells of the Basilica
toll for believers and non believers alike,
for the loved and the lonely,
for those whose stories are just beginning,
and those whose stories are closer to the end,

The river of sound washes over
everyone and everything,
on the miracle of this most ordinary day.

Prayer

In a quiet corner of the supermarket parking lot
an employee in red t-shirt
kneels on a piece of cardboard,
bows, then rises to speak the holy words,
his view of Mecca unimpeded
by the dumpster and unpainted wooden fence.

mnemonic

It is sometimes necessary
to walk along a moonlit riverbank
barefoot, on the sodden strip
where water meets land,
to remind oneself
that something in the mud
remembers the stars.

Distress Signal

An old man in a café sits with his two daughters
while the older sister, commander-in-chief,
outlines the afternoon's campaign.

When the three get up to leave
he stops at a carriage to admire a baby
and Sister General, focused on their next mission,
waggles her fingers to move him along.

As he shuffles obediently past my table
our eyes meet and he flashes
a silent S.O.S, a distress signal from a ship
beyond hope of rescue.

When Grief Comes Calling

Grief waits patiently for the phone to ring
to bring the midnight news that can't be borne,
but must be borne. Grief comes quietly
to the door, slips through the keyhole
like smoke, or the long tail of a bad dream
that wraps around you and won't let go.

When grief comes calling
try as you might you cannot bar
this uninvited guest who sours the milk,
turns each bite of food to sand and dust.

But as time passes, small pleasures begin their
slow, tip-toed return—the sound of dry leaves
dancing on the wind, or the smell of baking bread.

And then one night as you drive
over the crest of a hill a full moon,
lying low and huge in the sky, leaps into view
like a giant child playing hide and seek,
and in that moment of surprise and wonder
you cross the border of a new land
where grief still resides, but no longer rules.

Doppleganger
(for Carol)

Standing in the check-out line,
mind drifting, but jarred from waking sleep
by the sight of a woman who looked exactly like you,
the same slim, wiry frame and step-aside walk,
the same heart-shaped face framed by an undisciplined
shock of brown curls, the same half smile,
broadcasting both welcome and warning.

I couldn't look away, horrified and intrigued
at the thought our eyes might meet,
but your doppleganger
never even glanced my way.
There would have been nothing to see.
No thread of connection reaching
across the supermarket aisles to bind us
as I am bound to you,
gone these many years, and lying
quietly in the shade of a chestnut tree
atop a windblown hill.

Late that night I looked at your number
still in my phone, a digital ghost forever roaming
the corridors of cyber space, and for a moment
was tempted to call. If I did and heard your voice
what would I say?

And how would you answer?

Night Watch
(for Rachel)

The little cabinet you gave me
me so many years ago when you were moving,
the one that wouldn't fit in your new place,
still sits in my dining room, loaded with
incense and paper plates, books tucked
onto the shelves. You have never seen,
will never see it in its present home.

We lost touch soon after your move
when you disappeared, but I realize now
you had already disappeared,
the day you stood staring out a window
talking in a monotone about the estranged husband
who may or may not have actually existed,
the one who kept an army of Boston police on his payroll
to plant cameras all over town
that tracked your movements.
You turned away from the window
to ask if I worked for him as well.

That moment was the death
of any thought friendship might become
something more. Without speaking I put on my coat
for the long walk home after the last bus
and soon after that you entered the book
we all keep, the one filled with names
and faces of the vanished.

But last month, after those many years

I saw you sitting outside an all-night supermarket
in a shabby winter coat on a hot summer night
nestled inside a pile of shopping bags,
your portable home.

I called your name and you turned my way
with a doll's blank, glass-eyed stare
that turned to mild surprise when you
finally recognized my face. I mumbled some
foolish small talk that you ignored
and asked for money. When I handed you
a ten you smirked as if to say,
"That's the best you can do?"

I spared us both more useless words
and went on my way, left you to the vigil
for the ghosts that haunt your nights.

Young Woman, Dancing the Bolero

In the corner of the room,
in the humid night,
musicians sweat beneath a lantern's
pumpkin glow. The woman's partner
wraps his arm around her waist, guides
her across the rough wooded floor
in slow-quick rhythm.

For a moment their eyes lock,
then she turns away
to gaze into the distance,
as if peering through a mist
at a child playing with a doll,
a child whose image slowly fades,
replaced by a woman
walking on a road
veiled in shadow
toward destinations unknown.

after the storm haiku

snow-suited toddler
plows through piles of gleaming white
hot pink bowling ball

The Barn Raising
(a parable)

Last month, heat lightning struck my neighbor's barn.
We were in a dry spell, and the barn
burned like a pile of kindling.
Fire lit the night sky for miles; morning rose
on a pile of charred timbers.

I know my neighbor from church;
when his barn raising was announced
at Sunday service, he sat stiff-necked
and rigid—as if the lighting bolt
were proof he'd failed God's judgement.

The day of the raising was blessed
With a clear blue sky;
lumber had been hauled in the week before,
walls and rafters were all assembled
and lying ready on the ground.

And so fifty men began the dance
their fathers danced, and their fathers,
and theirs. Slowly the frame took shape.
As the day moved on, my neighbor's face,
an ice-bound stream, began to melt.

At last he climbed the final rafter,
and nailed a branch of Norway spruce.
The pastor said a prayer.

My neighbor raised his hammer like a sword.
A cheer rang through. At the clearing's edge,
a stand of oak trees spilled birds into the sky.

Memento Mori

I

According to legend a Roman general
who won a great battle would be paraded
through the city,
standing in a chariot, waving to the tens
of thousands lining the boulevard
cheering and shouting his name.
Behind him would stand a common soldier,
or sometimes a slave, holding a crown
above the general's head in a
gently mocking gesture and whispering in his ear,
to keep his vanity and pride in check,
"Remember . . . you must die."

II

There's a tiny bump on the back
of my right hand, invisible to the eye.
Years ago when I was being prepped
for brain surgery, a catheter
was inserted there and the bump remains.

Sometimes when I'm tired, or bored
or anxious, I'll realize
my finger has been moving over
it slowly, back and forth,
stroking it like a talisman,
a reminder to make the most
of the never-to-be-repeated day.

III
The late afternoon light that
slants through the blinds
painting zebra stripes
on the dining room table
takes me back to my sister's last day
when she lay in the hospital bed
and the sunlight streaming through the window
illuminated the salt-and-pepper hair
wispy and dry, spread out against her pillow.

Dreamtime

The tribesman standing on the Redline train
dressed in breechcloth only, body covered
with red and yellow paint, seems a long way from home,
and by "home" I mean not only the sun-seared
Australian landscape, but a long way from his time.

Yet I'm the one worried about time; to him
The idea of time means nothing. His people live
In the Dreamtime, where yesterday, today, tomorrow
Are but drops of water in a river without beginning or end.
It's the quantum physics of the outback, a wisdom that was
Ancient thousands of years before the pyramids were born.

It's a wisdom I find hard to appreciate on a rainy Tuesday morning
Before my second cup of coffee. I know, without knowing how
I know, that his presence is meant for me. No one else
can see him. The other passengers' ordinary faces are all
lit by the glow of their plastic toys.

Whatever message he carries for me, I don't want.
So I make a point of not meeting his eyes. I needn't bother;
He's not looking at me, or at anyone else on the train.
He's simply standing as the stations slip by
like beads on a prayer rope, and when I get off at Harvard Square
he doesn't acknowledge me in any way, just maintains
his silent vigil as the trains shoots down the dark tunnel.

But something has shifted, some portal cracked open.
Suddenly on the platform I see myself in first grade

at the little wooden desk, in clip-on tie
proudly clutching a newly sharpened pencil.
That image fades, and now I'm the young man about town,
admiring my reflection in a shop window as I pass,
hair-covered head empty as a paper cup.

That image fades, and now I'm watching my mother
being lowered into the ground.

That image fades, and now I see my eyes stare
out of a face lined with wrinkles. A finger beckons me near
I take one reluctant step forward, then another,
and softly, in a voice filled with dust,
he begins to speak.

A Conversation with My Younger Self

Congratulations to you, newly hatched grownup
in first solo apartment, boxes scattered
about like soldiers exhausted after a long march,
King Kong poster taped to the wall,
a little crooked, now guarding the kitchen.

The friends who helped you move are long gone,
empty beer bottles and pizza boxes all that remain.
Of course, hooking up the stereo
was your first priority and now Jimi Hendrix roars
through these little rooms like a low-flying fighter jet.

I peer at you through time's gauze curtain
and realize how much I want to say. I want
to tell you to go outside and look at the stars,
because sometimes it's good to feel small.

I want to tell you a woman's love is a precious thing,
not just a Saturday night's entertainment.

I want to tell you to turn down the stereo and call your mother.

I want to tell you all this and so much more,
but you can't hear a word I say, because this isn't
a conversation; it's the world's oldest bad joke,
and I'm the punch line, this white-haired ghost
brimming with after-the-fact wisdom, on a boat
pulling away from shore, sliding through dark water
to some destination unknown, hopping up and down

on one leg to get your attention, waving my arms
and shouting, as if what I'm saying
might actually make a difference.

And maybe you glance up for a moment
puzzled by some disturbance in the air
as you eat one last slice of cold pizza
off some dead grandmother's thrift shop dinner plate.

Every New Thing
(for Ann)

Every new thing is an act of treason,
a betrayal of the comfortable, the familiar.
An animal that has known only the cage
will cringe in the corner if the door
suddenly swings open, squealing on
ancient, rusted hinges.
If I have one wish for you, for me,
for us all, it's to remember that our own cages
are locked only by the fear of change,
that we have the power to shove those doors open
to take one step, then another,
into a new world.

The Author

Photo © Gordon Webster

Charles Coe's poetry and prose has appeared in numerous journals and magazines, and his poems have been set to music by composers Julia Carey, Beth Denisch and Robert Moran. His first poetry collection is *Picnic on the Moon* (Leapfrog Press) and his second is *All Sins Forgiven: Poems for My Parents* (Leapfrog Press). Charles also writes feature articles, book reviews and interviews for publications such as *Harvard Magazine, Northeastern University Law Review* and the *Boston Phoenix.* He is an adjunct professor of English in the Salve Regina low-residency MFA Program in Newport, Rhode Island. In addition to his work as a writer, he has an extensive background as a jazz vocalist and has performed and recorded with numerous musicians throughout New England.

CPSIA information can be obtained
at www.ICGtesting.com
Printed in the USA
LVHW111133260219
608522LV00006B/4/P

9 781948 585026